Quick &
Vegan No-Ba
Cook

CW00860218

Over 75 delicious recipes for cookies, fudge, bars, and other tasty treats!

By Susan Evans

Free Bonus!

Would you like to receive one of my cookbooks for free? Just leave me on honest review on Amazon and I will send you a digital version of the cookbook of your choice! All you have to do is email me proof of your review and the desired cookbook and format to susan.evans.author@gmail.com. Thank you for your support, and have fun cooking!

INTRODUCTION 1

MEASUREMENT CONVERSIONS 2

COOKIES AND BARS 3

Coconut Cookie Butter Sandwich Cookies 4
Almond Chocolate Bars...5
Coconut Date Bars..7
Granola Bites 8
Cookie Butter Coconut Haystacks.................................9
Raw Raspberry Bars 10
Skinny No Bake Cookies 12
Almond Joy Protein Bars...13
Homemade Peanut Butter Chocolate Lara Bars............15
Oatmeal Chocolate Cookies...16
Raw Chocolate Fudge Bars 17
Coconut Pumpkin Chocolate Bars................................18
Monster Granola Trail Mix Bars 19
Healthy Breakfast Cookies 20
Cinnamon Roll Protein Bars..21
5 minute Peanut Butter Granola Bars 22
Chocolate Blueberry Bars..23
Puppy Chow Bars...24
Peanut Butter Corn Flake Cookies 25

FUDGE AND PUDDING 26

Peanut Butter Fudge..27
Chocolate Pudding..28
Christmas Fudge...29

Chocolate Avocado Pudding..................................30
Raw Chocolate Pudding 31
Vegan Carrot Pudding...32
Quinoa Pudding...33
Avocado, Banana & Chocolate Pudding 34
Chocolate Pudding 2..35

CANDY 36

Raw Candy 37
Rock Candy 38
Orange and Lemon Peel Candy 39

SNACKS & APPETIZERS 40

Coffee Ice Cream with Banana and Peanuts..................41
Sweet Sticky Rice with Mangoes 42
Coconut Ice 43
Spiced Plantains and Pineapple............................44
Moroccan-Spiced Oranges 45
Chocolate-Covered Bananas 46
Apple and Pumpkin Dessert 47
Orange Poached Pears 48
Fried Cinnamon Strips 49
Apple and Pumpkin Dessert 50
Baked Apples...51
Poached Mint Peaches..52
Summer Berry Medley with Mint and Limoncello........53
Date Charoset..54

FRUIT SALADS & SOUPS 55

Strawberry Salad with Balsamic Vinegar *56*
Watercress, Melon and Almond Salad *57*
Frozen Berries Soup Salad *58*
Strawberry Tapioca *59*
Elderberry Soup *60*
Spicy Melon Soup *61*

FROZEN DESSERTS 62

Soda-Pop Ice Cream *63*
Watermelon Granita with Champagne *64*
Mint-Grapefruit Granita *65*
Lime & Basil Sorbet *66*
Chocolate-Hazelnut Soy Ice Cream *67*
Frozen Tropical Fruit Salad *68*
Pineapple Orange Sorbet *69*
Pineapple and Basil Sorbet *70*
Pink Grapefruit Blueberry Sorbet *71*
Peach and Strawberry Sorbet *72*
Coconut-Lime Sorbet *73*
Banana Ice Cream *74*
Cranberry Ice *75*

EVEN MORE DESSERTS! 76

Raw Brownies *77*
Whipped Coconut Cream *78*
Chocolate Almond Cherry Crisps *79*
Honey Peanut Butter Balls (Gluten-Free) *80*

Peppermint Patties (Gluten-Free) *81*
Chocolate Pretzel Peanut Butter Squares......................*82*
Thin Mint Puppy Chow *83*
Lemon Vanilla Energy Balls *84*
Peanut Butter Balls (Gluten-Free)...................................*85*
Peanut Butter Chocolate Haystacks................................*86*
Thin Mints...*87*
Sunflower and Pumpkin Seed Energy Balls...................*88*

THANK YOU **89**

INTRODUCTION

Everyone loves desserts, but sometimes it's just too hot to turn on the oven or we don't have the time to deal with the preparation baking requires. Furthermore, it's not always easy to find quality vegan recipes and when we do they can be intimidating for less experienced chefs. If your baking abilities prevent you from attempting delicious treats, let your fears of ruining a dessert go, and create some deliciously easy no-bake desserts! The following vegan recipes render preparing home-made treats simple and quick for everyone, from the busy mother to novice chef.

This no-bake cookbook contains everything you need to make perfect vegan desserts that will make everyone's mouth water. Impress your family and guests by presenting the perfect finish to a meal: a decadent dessert that requires no oven! From cookies, to fudge, to dessert bars, to candy, and other treats; there's something here for everyone to enjoy! So let's turn off that oven and let's get cooking!

MEASUREMENT CONVERSIONS

Liquid/Volume Measurements (approximate)

1 teaspoon = 1/6 fluid ounce (oz.) = 1/3 tablespoon = 5 ml

1 tablespoon = 1/2 fluid ounce (oz.) = 3 teaspoons = 15 ml

1 fluid ounce (oz.) = 2 tablespoons = 1/8 cup = 30 ml

1/4 cup = 2 fluid ounces (oz.) = 4 tablespoons = 60 ml

1/3 cup = 2⅔ fluid ounces (oz.) = 5 ⅓ tablespoons = 80 ml

1/2 cup = 4 fluid ounces (oz.) = 8 tablespoons = 120 ml

2/3 cup = 5⅓ fluid ounces (oz.) = 10⅔ tablespoons = 160 ml

3/4 cup = 6 fluid ounces (oz.) = 12 tablespoons = 180 ml

7/8 cup = 7 fluid ounces (oz.) = 14 tablespoons = 210 ml

1 cup = 8 fluid ounces (oz.) = 1/2 pint = 240 ml

1 pint = 16 fluid ounces (oz.) = 2 cups = 1/2 quart = 475 ml

1 quart = 4 cups = 32 fluid ounces (oz.) = 2 pints = 950 ml

1 liter = 1.055 quarts = 4.22 cups = 2.11 pints = 1000 ml

1 gallon = 4 quarts = 8 pints = 3.8 liters

Dry/Weight Measurements (approximate)

1 ounce (oz.) = 30 grams (g)

2 ounces (oz.) = 55 grams (g)

3 ounces (oz.) = 85 grams (g)

1/4 pound (lb.) = 4 ounces (oz.) = 125 grams (g)

1/2 pound (lb.) = 8 ounces (oz.) = 240 grams (g)

3/4 pound (lb.) = 12 ounces (oz.) = 375 grams (g)

1 pound (lb.) = 16 ounces (oz.) = 455 grams (g)

2 pounds (lbs.) = 32 ounces (oz.) = 910 grams (g)

1 kilogram (kg) = 2.2 pounds (lbs.) = 1000 gram (g)

COOKIES AND BARS

Coconut Cookie Butter Sandwich Cookies

SERVINGS: 24
PREP TIME: 10 min.
TOTAL TIME: 25 min.

Ingredients

- 48 toasted coconut cookie thins
- 1 cup crunchy cookie butter
- 20 oz. vanilla almond bark candy coating

Instructions

1. Line large baking pan with wax paper. On the bottom side of 24 cookies, spread a teaspoonful of cookie butter. Top each with another cookie (bottom side next to cookie butter) and press down lightly.
2. Place candy coating in large microwave-safe bowl and melt in microwave following directions on package. One cookie sandwich at a time, place in melted candy. Slightly move cookie around to make sure bottom is covered. Carefully spoon candy coating on cookie. Cover completely. Lift out with fork and gently tap fork on side of bowl to remove excess candy. Place on wax paper lined pan. Repeat with all cookies.
3. Place pan in refrigerator for about 15 minutes to set.

Almond Chocolate Bars

SERVINGS: 16
PREP TIME: 20 min.
TOTAL TIME: 1 hours 30 min

Ingredients

Crust:
- 1½ cup whole almonds
- 2 tablespoons coconut oil
- 2 tablespoons coconut nectar syrup
- 1 tablespoon almond butter or peanut butter
- ½ teaspoon cinnamon
- pinch of fine grain sea salt, to taste

Middle layer:
- 2 medium ripe bananas, peeled
- ¼ cup coconut oil, softened slightly
- 2 tablespoons almond butter or peanut butter
- 1 teaspoon pure vanilla extract
- pinch of fine grain sea salt, to taste

Chocolate drizzle:
- 3 tablespoons mini dark chocolate chips
- ½ tablespoon coconut oil

Instructions

1. Line an 8-inch square pan with two pieces of parchment paper, one going each way.
2. Process almonds in a food processor or blender until a fine crumb forms. Add the rest of the crust ingredients and process until mixed. The mixture should stick together when pressed with your fingers. If it does not, add a splash of water and process again for a couple of seconds.
3. Pour crust mix into prepared pan, pressing down firmly and smoothing evenly into pan. Place in freezer and go to next step.
4. Rinse food processor or blender. Add the middle layer ingredients into the processor and process until smooth. Remove crust from the freezer and pour this mix on top. Smooth out.

Return to freezer for at least 1-1½ hours or until the middle layer firm to the touch.

5. In a small pot, heat the chocolate and coconut oil on low heat. Stir to combine. When half chips have melted, remove the pot from the heat and stir until completely melted.

6. Remove the bars from the freezer. Lift out of the pan and slice into squares. Spread the squares on a plate lined with parchment paper.

7. Drizzle on melted chocolate and return bars to the freezer until the chocolate is firm.

8. Serve. Wrap leftovers and store in the freezer.

Coconut Date Bars

Ingredients

- ⅓ cup slivered almonds
- ½ cup flaked coconut
- 10 pitted dates
- ¼ cup cashews
- 1 teaspoon coconut oil

Instructions

1. Blend almonds and coconut in a food processor. Add dates and pulse until combined. Add cashews and coconut oil, pulsing until mixture is thick and sticks together.
2. Transfer to a sheet of waxed paper. Form into a square and fold sides of waxed paper over the top.
3. Refrigerate at least 30 minutes or until solid.

Granola Bites

SERVINGS: 24
PREP/TOTAL TIME: 10 min.

Ingredients

- 1 cup rolled oats
- 1 cup quick oats
- ¼ cup flour
- ½ cup peanut butter
- ½ cup honey
- ½ teaspoons salt
- ¼ cup dates
- ¼ cup craisins or chopped dried apricots
- ¼ cup walnuts

Instructions

1. Mix all ingredients together and stir until well combined.
2. Roll into about 24 balls. Refrigerate at least 15 minutes before serving.
3. Store in refrigerator.

Cookie Butter Coconut Haystacks

SERVINGS: 12
PREP TIME: 10 min.
TOTAL TIME: 15 min.

Ingredients

- ⅔ cup corn syrup
- 1 cup white chocolate chips
- ⅔ cup cookie butter
- dash of salt
- ½ teaspoons coconut extract
- 4 cups of cornflakes
- 1 cup toasted coconut

Instructions

1. In a large bowl, mix the cornflakes and toasted coconut. Set aside.
2. In a medium saucepan, heat together the corn syrup, white chocolate chips, and cookie butter. Once melted and heated together, allow it to simmer and slightly bubble for 2-3 minutes. Remove from heat and stir in salt and coconut extract.
3. Immediately pour heated mixture over cornflake/coconut mix in the large bowl and mix to coat evenly. It should be cool enough to handle after a few minutes.
4. Lay out a sheet of waxed paper and using your hands, form the cookie mix into generous "stacks" and allow them to completely cool.

Raw Raspberry Bars

SERVINGS: 7-10
PREP/ TOTAL TIME: 45 min.

Ingredients

Bottom Layer:
- ¾ cup oat flour
- 2 tablespoons water
- 1 tablespoon palm shortening or coconut oil
- 1 tablespoon maple syrup
- 1 tablespoon molasses

Blueberry Layer (Blue):
- 1 cup pureed organic blueberries
- 1½ cup oat flour
- ¼ cup maple syrup
- 3 tablespoons palm shortening or coconut oil

Oat Layer (White):
- ¾ cup oat flour
- 4 tablespoons water
- 1 tablespoon palm shortening or coconut oil
- 1 tablespoon white sugar

Raspberry Layer (Red):
- 1 cup pureed organic raspberries
- 1½ cup oat flour
- ¼ cup maple syrup
- 3 tablespoon palm shortening or coconut oil

Instructions

1. <u>Bottom Layer</u>: Melt shortening/coconut oil in microwave and combine with the additional ingredients, mixing well. Press into a thin layer in an 8×8 inch pan lined with parchment paper. Place in freezer.
2. <u>Blueberry Layer</u>: Puree blueberry in a food processor. Melt oil and combine remaining ingredients. Press on top of bottom layer. Place back into the freezer.

3. Oat layer: Melt oil in microwave and combine with other ingredients. Combine well. Press on top of blueberry layer. Place back into the freezer.
4. Raspberry layer: Puree raspberry in a food processor. Melt oil and combine all remaining ingredients. Press on top of oat layer.
5. Chill in refrigerator for at least 30 minutes before removing and cutting.
6. Garnish with cocoa power or chocolate shavings. Enjoy now or freeze for later.

Skinny No Bake Cookies

SERVINGS: 24 cookies
PREP TIME: 10 min.
TOTAL TIME: 40 min.

Ingredients

- ⅓ cup granulated sugar
- ¼ cup unsweetened cocoa powder
- ½ cup soy milk
- ¼ cup protein powder shake mix
- ½ cup creamy peanut butter
- 1 banana, mashed
- ½ teaspoons espresso powder
- 2 ½ cup quick cook oats
- 3 tablespoons mini semi-sweet morsels, for garnish (optional)

Instructions

1. Add sugar, cocoa, milk and protein powder in a medium saucepan over medium heat. Stir constantly until mixture starts to bubble slightly. Remove from heat and stir in peanut butter, banana and espresso powder. Fold in oats until fully combined.
2. Spoon onto parchment paper using a 2 tablespoons scoop. Using bottom of scoop or spoon to make a small indentation. Sprinkle a few mini morsels on top, pressing lightly with fingertips. Allow cookies to set, about 30 minutes.
3. Store cookies in airtight container in refrigerator for up to one week.

Almond Joy Protein Bars

SERVINGS: 12
PREP/TOTAL TIME: 30 min.

Ingredients

- 1 ¾ cups whole oats
- 2 cups quinoa, cooked
- ½ cup + ½ cup unsweetened shredded coconut, divided
- ⅛ cup ground flax seed
- ½ cup roughly chopped almonds
- ½ cup dark chocolate chips
- ⅔ cup honey
- ⅓ cup brown sugar
- pinch of salt
- ⅓ cup almond butter
- 1 teaspoon vanilla extract
- ½ teaspoon coconut extract

Instructions

1. Cut parchment paper to fit a 9×13 inch pan.
2. Combine oats, cooked quinoa, ½ cup coconut, flaxseed, almonds, and dark chocolate chips in a bowl and combine.
3. In a small saucepan over medium heat, combine honey, brown sugar and salt. Stir until it comes to a slight boil.
4. Remove from heat. Stir in the almond butter, coconut extract and vanilla until incorporated. Let it slightly cool, but keep warm enough to be pourable.
5. Pour warm mixture over the dry ingredients and mix until well combined. The chocolate will begin to melt. Work as quickly as possible to work the chocolate too much.
6. Add mix to the prepared pan and with a piece of parchment paper press down to even out the surface. Sprinkle remaining ½ cup of coconut on top of the bars, and press down with the back of a spoon.
7. Let completely cool down, then cool in the refrigerator for at least an hour before eating. Cut into bars, and store in an airtight

container, separating layers with parchment paper. Store in the refrigerator.

Homemade Peanut Butter Chocolate Lara Bars

SERVINGS: 16
PREP TIME: 5 min.
TOTAL TIME: 2 hours

Ingredients

- 2½ cups (410 grams) pitted dried dates
- ¾ cup unsalted peanuts
- 2 tablespoons unsweetened cocoa powder
- 1 oz. grated 100% cocoa chocolate
- ¼ teaspoons sea salt

Instructions

1. Line a 7x7 inch pan with plastic foil.
2. In a food processor place dates and pulse until they are finely chopped and form a ball.
3. Add peanuts, cocoa powder and salt. Pulse a few more times until the peanuts are finely chopped. While the food processor is still running, add the grated chocolate.
4. Take the date mixture out and spread it evenly in the prepared pan. Cover with more plastic foil and refrigerate for at least 2 hours before cutting into bars or squares.

Oatmeal Chocolate Cookies

SERVINGS: 24
PREP TIME: 5 min.
TOTAL TIME: 40 hours

Ingredients

- ⅔ cup maple syrup
- ¼ cup vegetable oil
- 5 tablespoons unsweetened cocoa powder
- 1 teaspoon ground cinnamon
- ½ cup peanut butter
- 1 cup rolled oats
- 1 teaspoon vanilla extract

Instructions

1. Combine maple syrup, oil, cocoa and cinnamon in a saucepan over medium heat. Boil for three minutes, constantly stirring. Remove from heat and stir in peanut butter, rolled oats and vanilla until it is well mixed.
2. Drop large spoonfuls onto waxed paper. Chill for 30 minutes.

Raw Chocolate Fudge Bars

SERVINGS: 8
PREP/TOTAL TIME: 15 min.

Ingredients

- ¾ cup/180g coconut oil
- ½ cup/120ml coconut butter
- ½ cup/60g cacao powder for raw or natural un-dutched (light) cocoa powder, sifted
- ½ cup/120ml maple syrup
- Pinch of fine sea salt or Himalayan salt
- ⅓ cup/17g freeze dried raspberries or other freeze dried berries
- ¼ cup/28g soaked and dehydrated raw almonds for raw or roasted almonds, coarsely chopped
- 2 tablespoons/20g cacao nibs
- Extra cacao powder for raw or natural un-dutched (light) cocoa powder, for dusting

Instructions

1. Line a pan with parchment paper and set aside.
2. In a medium bowl place the coconut oil and coconut butter into a bowl filled a quarter of the way up with hot water. Stir until both are fully melted.
3. Whisk in the sifted cacao powder until smooth and well mixed.
4. Whisk in the maple syrup and a pinch of salt until fully combined.
5. Mix in the freeze dried raspberries, chopped almonds and cacao nibs.
6. Pour into parchment-lined loaf pan. Leave in the fridge for at least 1 hour.
7. Cut into desired pieces and dust with additional cacao powder before serving.

Coconut Pumpkin Chocolate Bars

SERVINGS: 8
PREP TIME: 40 min.
TOTAL TIME: 40 min.

Ingredients

- 10 medjool dates, pitted and soaked for 15-30 minutes in water
- 1 cup almonds
- 1½ tablespoon dark, unsweetened cocoa powder
- 1½ teaspoon cinnamon, divided
- ¼ cup coconut butter, softened until spreadable
- 1 banana
- ¼ cup pumpkin puree
- 2 tablespoons honey
- unsweetened coconut flakes for garnish (optional)

Instructions

1. Combine dates, almonds, cocoa powder and ½ teaspoon cinnamon in a food processor. Process until a ball starts to form and dough becomes sticky.
2. Transfer to a 9×5 inch baking pan (a bread loaf pan). Spread and flatten out across the bottom of the entire pan.
3. Spread softened coconut butter as evenly as possible on top of the date/nut mix.
4. Add banana, pumpkin, honey and remaining cinnamon to food processor and process until smooth and fully combined.
5. Pour mix on top of the coconut butter, spreading evenly across the entire surface.
6. Sprinkle coconut flakes on top and freeze until set. About 30 minutes.
7. Cut into 8 squares once frozen.
8. Keep bars stored in the freezer.
9. Serve directly from the freezer or thawed for a couple of minutes for a softer pumpkin top layer.

Monster Granola Trail Mix Bars

SERVINGS: 12 bars
PREP TIME: 10 min.
TOTAL TIME: 1-2 hours

Ingredients

- ⅓ cup packed light brown sugar
- ¼ cup creamy peanut butter
- ¼ cup honey
- 4 tablespoons unsalted butter
- 2 cups quick oats
- ½ cup crispy rice cereal
- 1 cup Monster trail mix
- ¼ cup semisweet chocolate chips

Instructions

1. In a medium saucepan over medium-low heat, combine brown sugar, peanut butter, honey and butter; stirring frequently.
2. Bring sugar mix to a boil and then continue cooking for an additional 2-3 minutes. Stirring constantly until sugar dissolves. Stir in oats and crispy rice cereal until evenly coated.
3. Let mixture cool for 5 minutes.
4. Pick a handful of M&Ms from the trail mix and set aside.
5. Place parchment paper in an 8x8 inch baking dish.
6. Once mixture has cooled slightly, fold in trail mix and press into the prepared dish.
7. Sprinkle M&Ms and chocolate chips over the top of the bars and press bottom of a bowl or cup into the bars.
8. Place dish in refrigerator and let bars set up for 1-2 hours.
9. Cut bars and serve.

Healthy Breakfast Cookies

Ingredients

- ½ cup creamy peanut butter
- 2 tablespoons honey or agave nectar
- 1 teaspoon vanilla extract
- Pinch of salt, optional
- ½ cup Rice Krispie cereal
- ¼ cup flaxseed or sub oat flour
- ½ cup old-fashioned oats, uncooked
- Chocolate chips, if desired

Instructions

1. Combine the peanut butter, honey, vanilla, and salt in a medium-sized bowl. Microwave for 20-30 seconds and stir until combined.
2. In the same bowl, add in the rice Krispie cereal, flaxseed, and oats. Stir together until combined.
3. Form balls with the mix and then flatten the balls in your hand to create a cookie shape.
4. If desired, melt 3 tablespoons of chocolate chips in the microwave. Put the melted chocolate in a small Ziploc bag and cut a small hole in the tip of the bag. Drizzle the chocolate across the cookies and let the chocolate harden.
5. Store cookies in an airtight container for 4-5 days or freeze for up to 3 months.

Cinnamon Roll Protein Bars

SERVINGS: 12
PREP/ TOTAL TIME: 25 min.

Ingredients

- 1 cup raw, unsalted cashews
- 1 cup soft, pitted dates
- ¾ cup vanilla protein powder
- ½ teaspoons cinnamon
- ¼ teaspoons sea salt
- ½ cup rolled oats
- 1 tablespoon unsweetened almond milk (or favorite non-dairy milk)

Drizzle:
- 3 tablespoon vanilla protein powder
- 1 tablespoon almond milk (or favorite non-dairy milk)

Instructions

1. Place cashews and dates in a food processor or blender and process until they come together in a ball (about 2-3 minutes).
2. Break up ball and add in protein powder, oats, cinnamon and salt. Process until oats are broken up. Add in 1 tablespoon of milk and process until it comes together in a ball again.
3. Line an 8 x 8 baking dish with plastic wrap. Take the "dough" from food processor and spread out and flatten in baking dish.
4. Place in freezer for 15 minutes.
5. Meanwhile, make protein drizzle by combining the protein powder and non-dairy milk until powder has been absorbed.
6. Remove bars from freezer and lift out of dish by picking up the plastic wrap. Cut into 12 bars.
7. Add protein drizzle to a Ziploc bag and cut a very small hole in one corner. Pipe mixture in desired pattern over bars.
8. Place in baking dish and freeze for another 15 minutes or until drizzle has hardened.
9. Keep in fridge.

5 minute Peanut Butter Granola Bars

SERVINGS: 12
PREP/ TOTAL TIME: 10 min. + refrigeration

Ingredients

- 1¾ cup rolled oats
- 1 cup crisp puffed brown rice cereal
- ¼ cup pumpkin seeds
- ¼ cup sunflower seeds
- ¼ cup chia seeds or ⅛ cup finely ground flaxseed (both optional)
- ¼ cup unsweetened coconut (optional)
- ½ cup brown rice syrup
- ⅓ cup creamy peanut butter
- 1 teaspoon vanilla extract (optional)

Instructions

1. Add the dry ingredients to a large bowl. Combine and mix together.
2. In a microwave safe bowl, mix together the wet ingredients. Microwave for about 20 to 30 seconds.
3. Pour wet ingredients into dry and mix well. Place mixture into a shallow pan and flatten down. Place pan in fridge to let the bars set.
4. After at least 30 minutes in the fridge, cut them into bars and wrap them up in foil.
5. Store in the fridge.

Chocolate Blueberry Bars

SERVINGS: 12
PREP TIME: 5 min.
TOTAL TIME: 20 min.

Ingredients

- 2 cups of raw cashews (or any nut)
- 1 cup dried blueberries
- 1 cup pitted dates
- ½ teaspoons sea salt
- ⅓ cup dairy-free chocolate chips

Instructions

1. Add cashews to food processor and process until broken down, about 30 seconds.
2. Add in dried blueberries, dates and sea salt. Process until it comes together into a sticky ball.
3. Line a 9 x 9 inch baking pan with plastic wrap. Remove "dough" from food processor and place in baking pan. Flatten out "dough" making sure it is even and all corners are filled in. Place in freezer for 15 minutes.
4. Remove from freezer and lift plastic wrap out of pan. Cut into 12 bars.
5. In a microwave or double-boiler, melt chocolate. Add chocolate to a Ziploc bag and cut off a small corner. Squeeze chocolate out of bag in a zig-zag motion over bars.
6. Store in fridge up to several weeks.

Puppy Chow Bars

SERVINGS: 16
PREP/ TOTAL TIME: 10 min.

Ingredients

- 4 cups Chex cereal
- 5 marshmallows
- 1½ cup chocolate chips
- ¾ cup peanut butter
- powdered sugar

Instructions

1. In a large bowl, melt together marshmallows, chocolate chips, and peanut butter. Microwave at 50% power for 45 seconds at a time, stirring in between. Stir in Chex cereal once it has melted.
2. Press into 8x8 inch baking dish. Press well, so they stick together as a bar. Sift powdered sugar over the top.
3. Let cool completely before serving.

Peanut Butter Corn Flake Cookies

SERVINGS: 20
PREP TIME: 5 min.
TOTAL TIME: 15 min.

Ingredients

- 1 cup sugar
- 1 cup light corn syrup
- 1 cup creamy peanut butter
- 6 cup Corn Flakes cereal

Instructions

1. Heat sugar and syrup in a small saucepan, until the sugar dissolves. Do not boil. Remove from heat and stir in the peanut butter.
2. Put Corn Flakes in a large bowl and pour sugary mixture over them. Gently mix everything until coated, being careful not to smash up Corn Flakes.
3. Drop onto wax paper by the spoonful. Let them cool and set for a few minutes.

FUDGE AND PUDDING

Peanut Butter Fudge

SERVINGS: 24
PREP TIME: 10 min.
TOTAL TIME: 45 min.

Ingredients

- ¾ cup vegan margarine
- 1 cup peanut butter
- 3⅔ cups confectioners' sugar

Instructions

1. Lightly grease a 9 x 9 inch baking dish.
2. Melt margarine in a saucepan over low heat. Remove from heat. Stir in peanut butter until smooth. Gradually add and stir confectioners' sugar, until well mixed.
3. Pour into prepared pan and chill until firm. Cut into squares and serve.

Chocolate Pudding

SERVINGS: 4
PREP TIME: 5 min.
TOTAL TIME: 3 hours 30 min

Ingredients

- 2 tablespoons cornstarch
- 1 cup soy milk
- 1 cup soy creamer
- ½ cup white sugar
- 3 tablespoons egg replacer (dry)
- 3 oz. semisweet chocolate, chopped
- 2 teaspoons vanilla extract

Instructions

1. In a medium saucepan mix in cornstarch, soy milk and soy creamer. Stir until cornstarch is dissolved. Place on medium heat and stir in sugar. Whisking frequently until mixture begins to boil. Remove from heat.
2. In a small bowl whisk egg replacer with ¼ cup of hot milk mixture. Return to pan with remaining milk mixture. Cook over medium heat for 3 to 4 minutes, until thick. Make sure it is not boiling.
3. Place the chocolate in a medium bowl and pour in the hot milk mixture. Let stand for 30 seconds and stir until melted and smooth. Cool for 10 to 15 minutes. Stir in vanilla.
4. Pour into custard cups. Cover with plastic wrap and let cool at room temperature. Refrigerate for 3 hours or overnight.

Christmas Fudge

SERVINGS: 24
PREP TIME: 15 min.
TOTAL TIME: 50 min.

Ingredients

- ½ cup unsweetened cocoa powder
- ½ cup real maple syrup
- 1 teaspoon vanilla extract
- 1 pinch salt
- ½ cup refined coconut oil, melted
- ½ cup chopped walnuts
- 1 teaspoon unsweetened cocoa powder for dusting

Instructions

1. In a mixing bowl, stir in ½ cup cocoa powder, maple syrup, vanilla extract, and salt. Pour in melted coconut oil, stirring until thoroughly combined, coconut oil hardens, and the mixture becomes thick and grainy.
2. Place walnuts into a dry skillet over medium heat for 30 seconds to 1 minute; shaking skillet until walnuts are hot and aromatic. Turn off heat and let walnuts slightly cool, about 1 minute.
3. Stir warm walnuts into fudge and stir until smooth and glossy.
4. Pour fudge into a silicone ice cube mold. Scrape excess fudge back into the mixing bowl. Smooth the tops of the fudge pieces.
5. Wrap mold in plastic wrap and freeze, at least 30 minutes or until fudge is firm. Remove plastic wrap and remove each fudge piece out of the mold.
6. Dust pieces with 1 teaspoon cocoa powder before serving. Serve cold and freeze leftovers.

Chocolate Avocado Pudding

SERVINGS: 4
PREP TIME: 10 min.
TOTAL TIME: 40 min.

Ingredients

- 2 large avocados-peeled, pitted, and cubed
- ½ cup unsweetened cocoa powder
- ½ cup brown sugar
- ⅓ cup coconut milk
- 2 teaspoons vanilla extract
- 1 pinch ground cinnamon

Instructions

1. In a blender, blend avocados, cocoa powder, brown sugar, coconut milk, vanilla extract, and cinnamon until smooth.
2. Refrigerate pudding, about 30 minutes or until chilled.

Raw Chocolate Pudding

SERVINGS: 4
PREP TIME: 10 min.
TOTAL TIME: 1 hour 10 min

Ingredients

- 1 avocado-peeled, pitted, and cut into chunks
- 1 banana, peeled and cut into chunks
- 1 cup unsweetened soy milk
- ¼ cup raw cocoa powder
- 2 tablespoons agave nectar
- 1 teaspoon lemon juice
- ¼ cup shredded unsweetened coconut (optional)

Instructions

1. Place avocado, banana, soy milk, cocoa powder, agave nectar, lemon juice, and coconut into a blender. Cover. Puree until smooth.
2. Divide into small containers, and store in the refrigerator for at least 1 hour or until set.

Vegan Carrot Pudding

SERVINGS: 4
PREP TIME: 10 min.
TOTAL TIME: 45 min.

Ingredients

- 1 cup vanilla soy milk
- 2 tablespoons turbinado sugar
- 1½ teaspoons blackstrap molasses
- 1 teaspoon vanilla extract
- ½ teaspoon ground cinnamon
- ¼ teaspoon ground ginger
- ¼ teaspoon ground allspice
- ⅛ teaspoon ground nutmeg
- 2 tablespoons all-purpose flour
- ⅓ cup raisins
- ⅓ cup chopped walnuts
- 2 cups shredded carrots

Instructions

1. In a saucepan over medium-low heat, whisk soy milk, turbinado sugar, molasses, vanilla extract, cinnamon, ginger, allspice, and nutmeg until well incorporated, 2 to 3 minutes. Whisk in flour another 3 to 5 minutes until smooth.
2. Fold raisins and walnuts into soy milk mixture. Add carrots. Cook and stir pudding over low heat, keeping from boiling, until carrots are softened, around 30 minutes.

Quinoa Pudding

SERVINGS: 6
PREP TIME: 5 min.
TOTAL TIME: 40 min.

Ingredients

- 1 cup quinoa
- 2 cups water
- 2 cups apple juice
- 1 cup raisins
- 2 tablespoons lemon juice
- 1 teaspoon ground cinnamon, or to taste
- salt to taste
- 2 teaspoons vanilla extract

Instructions

1. Place quinoa in a sieve and thoroughly rinse. Drain then place in a medium saucepan with water. Over high heat, bring to a boil. Lower heat, cover the pan with lid, and simmer about 15 minutes or until all water is absorbed and quinoa is soft.
2. Add and mix in apple juice, raisins, lemon juice, cinnamon, and salt. Cover pan and simmer for 15 more minutes. Stir in vanilla extract. Serve warm.

Avocado, Banana & Chocolate Pudding

SERVINGS: 6
PREP TIME: 10 min.
TOTAL TIME: 1 hour 10 min.

Ingredients

- 1 ripe avocado, peeled and pitted
- 4 very ripe bananas
- ¼ cup unsweetened cocoa powder, plus more for garnish

Instructions

1. In a blender, blend avocados, bananas, and cocoa powder until smooth.
2. Pour into serving bowls and sprinkle additional cocoa powder on top.
3. Chill in refrigerator for at least 1 hour. Serve.

Chocolate Pudding 2

SERVINGS: 2
PREP TIME: 10 min.
TOTAL TIME: 45 min.

Ingredients

- 3 tablespoons cornstarch
- 2 tablespoons water
- 1½ cups soy milk
- ¼ teaspoon vanilla extract
- ¼ cup white sugar
- ¼ cup unsweetened cocoa powder

Instructions

1. In small bowl, form a paste by combining cornstarch and water.
2. In large saucepan over medium heat, stir soy milk, vanilla, sugar, cocoa and cornstarch mixture. Stir constantly until mixture boils and continue to stir until it thickens. Remove from heat.
3. Allow to cool five minutes and thicken. Chill in refrigerator until completely cool.
4. Serve.

CANDY

Raw Candy

SERVINGS: 40
PREP/TOTAL TIME: 20 min.

Ingredients

- 1 cup raisins
- 1 cup walnuts
- 1 tablespoon vegetable oil
- 1 cup sliced almonds

Instructions

1. In a blender or food processor, blend raisins and walnuts together until they form a sticky ball.
2. Coat your hands with oil and roll the mixture into marble sized balls. Coat with sliced almonds.
3. Cover and refrigerate up to 3 days.

Rock Candy

SERVINGS: 24
PREP TIME: 20 min.
TOTAL TIME: 10 days

Ingredients

- 6 cups cold water
- 6 cups white sugar

Instructions

1. Place water in a large bowl. Gradually add and dissolve sugar in the water, stirring until completely dissolved. Pour sugar water into clean jar and place a wooden skewer in the jar, making sure the top sticks out from the water. Cover with a cloth, and place jar in a cool place away from bright lights. Do not disturb crystals and leave it for several days until water is evaporated and crystals have formed on skewer.

Orange and Lemon Peel Candy

SERVINGS: 12
PREP TIME: 10 min.
TOTAL TIME: 4 hours 40 min

Ingredients

- 6 lemon peels, cut into ¼ inch strips
- 4 orange peels, cut into ¼ inch strips
- 2 cups white sugar
- 1 cup water
- ⅓ cup white sugar

Instructions

1. In large saucepan, add the lemon and orange peels and cover with water. Boil over high heat for 20 minutes. Drain and set aside.
2. Combine 2 cups sugar and 1 cup of water in medium saucepan. Bring to a boil and cook until a small amount dropped in cold water forms a soft thread. Add and stir in peels, reduce heat. Simmer 5 minutes and stir frequently. Drain.
3. Roll peel pieces, a couple at a time, in remaining sugar. Dry on wire rack for several hours. Store in airtight container.

SNACKS & APPETIZERS

Coffee Ice Cream with Banana and Peanuts

SERVINGS: 4
PREP TIME: 7 min.

Ingredients

- 2 cups vanilla low-fat ice cream
- 2 medium bananas, sliced
- ½ cup hot brewed espresso
- 2 tablespoons chopped, dry-roasted peanuts
- 2 tablespoons chocolate curls (about ½ oz.)

Instructions

1. Spoon ½ cup ice cream into each of 4 bowls. Top each serving with half of banana, 2 tablespoons espresso, 1 ½ teaspoons peanuts, and 1 ½ teaspoons chocolate.

Sweet Sticky Rice with Mangoes

SERVINGS: 6
PREP TIME: 15 min.
TOTAL TIME: 1 hour 35 min.

Ingredients

- 2 cups uncooked glutinous (sticky) white rice, rinsed
- 1 (13.5 oz.) can coconut milk, divided
- 1 cup white sugar
- 1 tablespoon white sugar
- ¼ teaspoon salt
- ¾ teaspoon cornstarch
- 2 ripe mangoes, peeled and cubed

Instructions

1. Cover rice with several inches of fresh water. Stand for 30 minutes. Drain so rice is covered by only ¼ inch of water.
2. Place rice in a microwave oven, cover, and cook on High for about 10 minutes or until the water has been absorbed and the rice is still wet. Stir and cook an additional 4 minutes or until almost dry.
3. Mix half the coconut milk and 1 cup of sugar in a bowl and stir to dissolve the sugar. Pour mixture over rice and stir until rice is coated with the mixture. Cover and allow the rice to stand at room temperature for 20 minutes.
4. Pour remaining ½ can of coconut milk into a saucepan and whisk in 1 tablespoon of sugar, salt, and cornstarch until smooth. Bring mixture to a simmer about 2 minutes over medium heat, constantly whisk, until thickened. Remove from heat and cool.
5. Scoop the rice into individual serving bowls and top each with 2 tablespoons of the coconut sauce and mango pieces.

Coconut Ice

SERVINGS: 20
PREP TIME: 5 min.
TOTAL TIME: 1 hour 30 min

Ingredients

- 2 cups white sugar
- ⅔ cup water
- 1 teaspoon vanilla extract
- 1 ½ cups flaked coconut
- 2 drops red food coloring

Instructions

1. Line a 7 x 7 inch pan with waxed paper or parchment. In a medium saucepan, combine and heat sugar and water on medium heat until sugar has dissolved. Bring to a boil and cook until syrup dropped in a glass of cold water forms a soft ball.
2. Remove from heat and immediately add and stir in vanilla and coconut. Stir 5 to 10 minutes or until mix begins to thicken.
3. Pour half of the mixture into the prepared pan and with a knife or spatula, level the surface. Stir in the food coloring to the other half of the mixture. Pour the pink mixture on top of other layer, and level the surface. With the back of a spoon, press all down firmly and allow to harden. When firm, turn out of the pan, remove the paper and cut into squares.

Spiced Plantains and Pineapple

SERVINGS: 4
PREP TIME: 5 min.
TOTAL TIME: 10 min.

Ingredients

- 2 ripe plantains (yellow and black skin), peeled and cut into 1 inch rounds
- 1 (20 oz.) can pineapple chunks in juice, drained, juice reserved
- 1 teaspoon ground cinnamon
- ¾ teaspoon ground nutmeg
- ¾ teaspoon ground cloves

Instructions

1. Heat a large skillet over medium heat and coat with cooking spray. Arrange plantain slices on the skillet in a single layer. Season with half of the cinnamon, nutmeg and cloves. Cook 2 to 3 minutes or until golden brown on the bottom. Turn over the slices and pour in the pineapple and a small amount of the juice. Sprinkle the remaining spices over the top and cook another 3 minutes or until browned on the bottom.

Moroccan-Spiced Oranges

SERVINGS: 4
PREP TIME: 5 min.
TOTAL TIME: 20 min.

Ingredients

- 2½ cups orange sections, cut into ½-inch pieces (about 6)
- ¼ cup slivered almonds
- 2 ½ tablespoons chopped pitted dates (about 4)
- 1 tablespoon powdered sugar
- 1 tablespoon fresh lemon juice
- ¼ teaspoon ground cinnamon
- Ground cinnamon (optional)
- Grated orange rind (optional)

Instructions

1. In a medium saucepan over medium heat, combine first 6 ingredients, tossing to combine.
2. Cover and chill 20 minutes. Garnish with cinnamon and rind, if desired.

Chocolate-Covered Bananas

SERVINGS: 6
PREP TIME: 20 min.
TOTAL TIME: 40 min.

Ingredients

- 8 oz. semisweet chocolate, chopped
- 6 popsicle sticks or wooden skewers
- 2 bananas, peeled and cut crosswise into thirds
- ⅓ cup coarsely chopped salted peanuts

Instructions

1. Place chocolate in a heatproof bowl set over (not inside) a pan of simmering water. Stir until melted.
2. Line a baking sheet with waxed paper. Insert a Popsicle stick in one end of each banana piece. Dip bananas in chocolate, one at a time, and spoon on additional chocolate to cover.
3. Sprinkle bananas with peanuts, and set on prepared baking sheet.
4. Refrigerate at least 20 minutes, or until chocolate is firm.

Apple and Pumpkin Dessert

Ingredients

- 2 (1 gram) packets sugar substitute
- 1 teaspoon pumpkin pie spice
- 1 Granny Smith apple - peeled, cored and chopped
- 1/4 cup canned pumpkin
- 2 tablespoons water

Instructions

1. In a microwave-safe bowl combine 1/3 packet of sugar substitute and 1/3 teaspoon pumpkin pie spice. Layer 1/4 of the apple pieces into the bowl and repeat. Spread pumpkin over the apples. Sprinkle the remaining sugar substitute and pumpkin pie spice on the pumpkin. Top with the remaining apples.
2. Pour water over the mixture.
3. Cook in microwave for 3½ minutes, stirring every minute.

Orange Poached Pears

SERVINGS: 3
PREP TIME: 15 min.
TOTAL TIME: 1 hour 45 min.

Ingredients

- 1½ cups orange juice without pulp
- ½ cup packed brown sugar
- ¼ cup white sugar
- 1 tablespoon vanilla extract
- 1 teaspoon ground cinnamon
- 3 whole pears, peeled and cored
- ½ cup chopped walnuts

Instructions

1. In a large saucepan, mix together orange juice, brown and white sugar, vanilla extract, and cinnamon over medium heat. Bring to a boil, and stir until sugar is dissolved. Place pears in syrup, and cover. Simmer pears for 1 hour and 15 minutes, while spooning sauce every 10 minutes over pears, and turning pears twice.
2. Transfer pears to individual serving dishes.
3. Continue cooking syrup, about 15 more minutes, constantly stirring until thickened. Mix in the walnuts.
4. Pour the sauce over the pears and serve.

Fried Cinnamon Strips

SERVINGS: 36
PREP TIME: 10 min.
TOTAL TIME: 30 min.

Ingredients

- 1 cup white sugar
- 1 teaspoon ground cinnamon
- ¼ teaspoon ground nutmeg
- 10 (8 inch) flour tortillas
- 3 cups oil for frying

Instructions

1. Combine sugar, cinnamon and nutmeg in a large re-sealable plastic bag. Seal and toss to mix ingredients.
2. Heat oil in deep-fryer or deep skillet. Fry 4 or 5 tortilla strips on a side, for 30 seconds until golden brown. Drain on paper towels.
3. While still warm, place the fried tortillas in bag and shake to coat with sugar mixture.
4. Serve immediately or store in an airtight container.

Apple and Pumpkin Dessert

SERVINGS: 1
PREP TIME: 5 min.
TOTAL TIME: 10 min.

Ingredients

- 2 (1 gram) packets sugar substitute
- 1 teaspoon pumpkin pie spice
- 1 Granny Smith apple-peeled, cored and chopped
- ¼ cup canned pumpkin
- 2 tablespoons water

Instructions

1. In the bottom of a microwave-safe bowl, sprinkle ⅓ packet of sugar substitute and ⅓ teaspoon pumpkin pie spice. Layer ¼ of the apple pieces into the bowl and repeat. Spread the pumpkin over the apples. Sprinkle the remaining sugar substitute and pumpkin pie spice on the pumpkin. Top with the remaining apples.
2. Pour water over the mixture.
3. Cook in microwave on high for 3½ minutes, and stir every minute.

Baked Apples

SERVINGS: 1
PREP TIME: 5 min.
TOTAL TIME: 15 min

Ingredients

- 1 Granny Smith apple, cored
- 1 tablespoon brown sugar
- ¼ teaspoon ground cinnamon

Instructions

1. Fill the core of the apple with the brown sugar and cinnamon. Wrap apple heavy foil, and twist extra foil into a tail for a handle.
2. Place apple in the coals of a campfire or barbeque and let cook 5 to 10 minutes, until softened.
3. Remove and unwrap, careful of not burning yourself with the hot sugar.

Poached Mint Peaches

Ingredients

- 6 firm, ripe peaches
- 2 cups sugar
- 1 vanilla bean, split (or ½ teaspoon pure vanilla extract)
- 2 strips lemon zest
- 1 large mint sprig, plus more for serving
- 4 cups water

Instructions

1. Lightly carve an X into bottom of peaches using a paring knife. In a large saucepan, combine sugar, vanilla, lemon zest, mint, and water. Cook over medium heat, about 2 minutes or until sugar has dissolved, stirring occasionally.
2. Add peaches and cover with water. Barely simmer for about 6 to 10 minutes, turning occasionally, until peaches are soft enough to easily pierce with a skewer.
3. Remove peaches and let slightly cool. Peel peaches using a paring knife and return to syrup.
4. Serve with mint sprigs.

Summer Berry Medley with Mint and Limoncello

SERVINGS: 6
PREP TIME: 5 min.
TOTAL TIME: 20 min.

Ingredients

- 1 cup fresh raspberries
- 2 cups fresh blackberries
- 2 cups hulled fresh strawberries, quartered
- 2 cups fresh blueberries
- ¼ cup sugar
- 1 tablespoon grated lemon rind
- 2 tablespoons fresh lemon juice
- 2 tablespoons limoncello (lemon-flavored liqueur)
- ½ cup torn mint leaves

Instructions

1. Combine first 8 ingredients in a bowl and let stand 20 minutes.
2. Gently stir in mint using a rubber spatula.
3. Serve.

Date Charoset

SERVINGS: 40
PREP TIME: 45 min.
TOTAL TIME: 2 hours 15 min.

Ingredients

- ½ pound chopped dates
- 1 cup golden raisins
- ½ cup red wine
- ½ cup coarsely chopped walnuts
- 1 teaspoon ground cinnamon
- ½ cup confectioners' sugar

Instructions

1. In a small saucepan, combine dates, raisins, and wine. Cook over low heat, and stir occasionally, until fruit thickens to a soft paste. Cool.
2. Stir nuts and cinnamon into the fruit mixture.
3. Form paste into small, bite-size balls. Roll in confectioners' sugar.
4. Serve.

FRUIT SALADS & SOUPS

Strawberry Salad with Balsamic Vinegar

SERVINGS: 6
PREP TIME: 10 min.
TOTAL TIME: 1 hour 10 min.

Ingredients

- 16 oz. fresh strawberries, hulled and large berries cut in half
- 2 tablespoons balsamic vinegar
- ¼ cup white sugar
- ¼ teaspoon freshly ground black pepper, or to taste

Instructions

1. Place strawberries in a bowl and drizzle vinegar over strawberries. Sprinkle with sugar. Stir gently. Cover, and let sit at room temperature for between 1 and 4 hours.
2. Grind pepper over berries before serving.

Watercress, Melon and Almond Salad

Ingredients

- 3 tablespoons fresh lime juice
- 1 teaspoon white sugar
- 1 teaspoon minced fresh ginger root
- ¼ cup vegetable oil
- 2 bunches watercress, trimmed and chopped
- 2½ cups cubed watermelon
- 2½ cups cubed cantaloupe
- ⅓ cup toasted and sliced almonds

Instructions

1. In a large bowl, whisk together lime juice, sugar, and ginger. Gradually add oil and season with salt and pepper.
2. Add watercress, watermelon, and cantaloupe to dressing. Toss to coat.
3. Transfer salad to plates. Sprinkle with sliced almonds.
4. Serve immediately.

Frozen Berries Soup Salad

SERVINGS: 5
PREP/TOTAL TIME: 2 hours.

Ingredients

- ½ cup barley
- 6 cups water
- ½ cup white sugar
- 1 (10 oz.) package frozen raspberries
- ½ cup raisins
- 1 cup pitted cherries

Instructions

1. In a large bowl, soak the barley overnight in the water.
2. In a large saucepan simmer the barley for 1 hour over low heat. Add sugar, raspberries and raisins and simmer for another 30 minutes. Add cherries and simmer for another 15 minutes or until the soup becomes thick.
3. Chill in the refrigerator and serve cold.

Strawberry Tapioca

SERVINGS: 4
PREP TIME: 10 min.
TOTAL TIME: 30 min.

Ingredients

- ½ cup fresh strawberries, hulled and halved
- 1½ cups water
- ¼ cup quick-cooking tapioca

Instructions

1. In a food processor or blender, blend strawberries and water until smooth. Pour into a small saucepan. Add and stir in tapioca. Let stand for 10 minutes or until softened. Bring to a boil over medium heat, stir frequently to prevent sticking. Remove when thick.
2. Pour into serving dishes.

Elderberry Soup

SERVINGS: 4
PREP TIME: 25 min.
TOTAL TIME: 45 min.

Ingredients

- 5 oz. elderberries
- 1 quart water, divided
- 1½ teaspoons cornstarch
- ½ pound apples-peeled, cored and diced
- 1 lemon peel
- white sugar, to taste

Instructions

1. In a pot, place elderberries with 2 cups water and bring to a boil. Reduce heat to low and simmer 10 minutes. Remove from heat, puree in a blender until smooth. Return to the pot. In a small bowl, mix cornstarch with 1 tablespoon of the puree. Stir back into the pot to thicken.
2. In a separate pot, bring apples and remaining water to a boil. Place the lemon peel in the pot. Reduce heat to low and simmer 10 minutes. Remove the lemon peel. Mix the elderberry puree into the apple mixture. Sweeten to taste with sugar.

Spicy Melon Soup

Ingredients

- 4 cups casaba melon, seeded and cubed
- ¾ cup coconut milk
- 2 lime juice
- 1 tablespoon freshly grated ginger
- 1 pinch salt

Instructions

1. In a food processor, combine casaba melon, coconut milk, lime juice, ginger, and salt. Process for 1 to 2 minutes or until the mixture is smooth.
2. Serve.

FROZEN DESSERTS

Soda-Pop Ice Cream

SERVINGS: 2
PREP/TOTAL TIME: 5 min.

Ingredients

- 1½ cups snow
- ¾ (12 oz.) can cola-flavored carbonated beverage

Instructions

1. In a medium bowl, combine and stir snow and cola.
2. Serve immediately.

Watermelon Granita with Champagne

SERVINGS: 4
PREP TIME: 15 min.
TOTAL TIME: 2 hours 15 min.

Ingredients

- 2 pounds watermelon, seeded and cubed
- ½ cup white sugar
- 1 cup champagne
- 4 slices watermelon

Instructions

1. Place cubed watermelon and sugar in a blender. Blend for 1 minute. Stir in the champagne. Pour this mixture into a plastic container. Cover and place in the freezer. Stir mixture with a fork every 30 minutes until frozen, for about 2 hours.
2. Before serving, remove the frozen granita from the freezer and stir well using a fork or process in the food processor until the desired consistency is reached.
3. Serve in tall glasses garnished with sliced watermelon.

Mint-Grapefruit Granita

SERVINGS: 4
PREP TIME: 20 min.
TOTAL TIME: 6 hour 20 min.

Ingredients

- ½ cup sugar
- ¼ cup packed fresh mint leaves, plus more for garnish
- 2 cups fresh grapefruit juice (about 3 medium grapefruits), strained
- ¼ cup fresh lemon juice (about 2 lemons), strained

Instructions

1. In a small saucepan, combine sugar, mint, and ½ cup water. Bring to a boil over medium-high heat, and stir often until sugar dissolves, about 3 to 5 minutes.
2. In a blender, combine fruit juices and mint syrup. Puree for 30 seconds on high. Pour into a shallow 2-quart baking dish. Freeze overnight or until solid.
3. Break granita into large chunks with a fork. Pulse in a food processor to form small crystals.
4. Serve immediately, with mint leaves, or cover and freeze up to 2 hours.

Lime & Basil Sorbet

SERVINGS: 8
PREP TIME: 30 min.
TOTAL TIME: 2 hours 35 min.

Ingredients

- 1 cup sugar
- 1 cup water
- ¾ cup fresh lime juice
- 20 fresh basil leaves, minced

Instructions

1. In a medium saucepan, bring water and sugar to a simmer over medium high heat until sugar is dissolved. Remove from heat.
2. Combine and puree syrup, lime juice, and basil in a blender. Pour the mixture in a container. Cover and store in freezer about 2 hours or until completely frozen.
3. Break frozen mixture into pieces and place in the blender. Blend until smooth. Return to the container and cover.
4. Store in freezer until ready to serve.

Chocolate-Hazelnut Soy Ice Cream

SERVINGS: 4
PREP TIME: 10 min.
TOTAL TIME: 6 hours 10 min.

Ingredients

- ½ (12 oz.) package extra-firm silken tofu
- 1 cup soy milk
- 1 tablespoon hazelnut flavored syrup
- 4 teaspoons instant espresso powder
- 1 teaspoon vanilla extract
- ⅔ cup semisweet chocolate chips, melted

Instructions

1. In a blender, combine tofu, soy milk, hazelnut syrup, espresso powder, and vanilla extract. Cover and puree until smooth. Pour in the melted chocolate, and puree until evenly mixed. Pour the mixture into a bowl and cover. Refrigerate at least 1 hour or until cold.
2. Pour the cold mixture into an ice cream maker and freeze according to the manufacturer's directions. When ice cream has thickened, remove it from the ice cream maker and transfer it to a container. Freeze 4 hours or overnight before serving.
3. Alternatively, cover and store in freezer about 2 hours or until completely frozen.

Frozen Tropical Fruit Salad

SERVINGS: 6
PREP TIME: 15 min.
TOTAL TIME: 1 hour 15 min.

Ingredients

- ½ cup white sugar
- 2 cups water
- 1 (6 oz.) can frozen orange juice concentrate, thawed
- 1 (6 oz.) can frozen lemonade concentrate, thawed
- 4 bananas, sliced
- 1 (20 oz.) can crushed pineapple with juice
- 1 (10 oz.) package frozen strawberries, thawed

Instructions

1. Dissolve sugar in the water. Add orange juice, lemonade, bananas, crushed pineapple with juice, strawberries and mix.
2. Pour into 9 x13 inch glass pan. Freeze until solid. When ready to serve, let it sit out for about 5 minutes before attempting to cut.

Pineapple Orange Sorbet

SERVINGS: 10
PREP TIME: 20 min.
TOTAL TIME: 3 hours

Ingredients

- ½ cup water
- ½ cup granulated sugar
- 2 cups orange juice
- 1 tablespoon lemon juice
- 1 (20 oz.) can crushed pineapple
- 2 teaspoons freshly grated orange zest

Instructions

1. In a medium saucepan, bring water and sugar over medium high heat to a simmer until sugar is dissolved.
2. Puree pineapple with its juice until smooth in a food processor or blender. Transfer to a metal bowl, and stir in syrup, lemon juice, orange juice, and orange zest. Freeze until slightly firm, but not completely frozen.
3. Process mixture in the food processor or blend in a blender until smooth.
4. Transfer to a container and freeze about 2 hours or until firm. Serve.

Pineapple and Basil Sorbet

SERVINGS: 16
PREP TIME: 20 min.
TOTAL TIME: 9 hours

Ingredients

- 1 pineapple-peeled, cored, and cut into chunks
- ½ cup white sugar
- ½ cup pineapple juice
- ¼ cup basil leaves

Instructions

1. In a blender, blend pineapple, sugar, pineapple juice, and basil until smooth. Refrigerate for 1 hour.
2. Place mix in an ice cream maker and mix according to manufacturer's Instructions. Or alternatively, pour the mixture into a container, and freeze 3 to 4 hours or until solid. Thoroughly stir the sorbet breaking up the ice crystals into a slushy consistency, and return to freezer until firm, about 3 hours.
3. Store in the freezer in a covered container. Freeze overnight.

Pink Grapefruit Blueberry Sorbet

Ingredients

- 3 cups fresh pink grapefruit juice
- 3 cups fresh or frozen blueberries
- 1½ cups white sugar, or to taste

Instructions

1. In a blender, pour grapefruit juice, blueberries, and sugar. Blend 2 to 3 minutes or until the sugar is dissolved and mixture is smooth.
2. Pour mixture into a container, and freeze 3 to 4 hours or until solid. Stir the sorbet to a slushy consistency, and return to freezer about 3 hours or until firm.
3. Pour into an airtight container. Freeze overnight.

Peach and Strawberry Sorbet

Ingredients

- 2 cups sliced fresh peaches
- 1 cup fresh strawberries, hulled
- 1 cup fresh orange juice
- ¼ cup brown sugar

Instructions

1. Place peaches, strawberries, orange juice, and brown sugar in a food processor. Puree until smooth.
2. Pour mixture into an ice cream maker and freeze according to manufacturer's Instructions until firm. Or alternatively, cover and store in freezer about 2 hours or until completely frozen.
3. Break frozen mix into pieces and place in the blender. Blend until smooth. Return to the container and cover.
4. Store in freezer until ready to serve.

Coconut-Lime Sorbet

SERVINGS: 4
PREP/TOTAL TIME: 30 min.

Ingredients

- 1 (15 oz.) can cream of coconut
- ½ cup fresh lime juice
- ¾ cup water

Instructions

1. Combine cream of coconut, lime juice, and water in the container of an ice cream maker. Freeze according to manufacturer's instructions. Alternatively, combine and puree the cream of coconut, lime juice, and water in a blender. Pour the mixture in a container. Cover and store in freezer about 2 hours or until completely frozen.
2. Break frozen mixture into pieces and place in the blender. Blend until smooth. Return to the container and cover.
3. Store in freezer until ready to serve.

Banana Ice Cream

SERVINGS: 2
PREP/TOTAL TIME: 10 min.

Ingredients

- 2 large frozen bananas, cut into small chunks
- 1 cup unsweetened almond milk
- 1 tablespoon chopped pecans
- 1 pinch ground cinnamon, or to taste

Instructions

1. Blend bananas, almond milk, pecans, and cinnamon together in a blender or food processor until creamy and smooth.

Cranberry Ice

SERVINGS: 12
PREP/TOTAL TIME: 45 min.

Ingredients

- 2 (12 oz.) packages fresh cranberries
- 2 cups white sugar
- 1¼ cups fresh orange juice
- 1 cup fresh lemon juice

Instructions

1. In a large pot, add cranberries and enough water to cover. Boil until cranberries begin to pop. Drain and put through a food mill placed over a large bowl.
2. While still warm add sugar to dissolve in the warm berries. The amount of sugar may vary depending on the tartness of the berries, so if you decide to add more sugar remember that the mixture will be tarter when it has been frozen.
3. After dissolving sugar in the berries, stir in fresh squeezed orange juice and fresh squeezed lemon juice. Pour in 8 or 9 inch square pan and freeze overnight. Take out of the freezer 5-10 minutes before cutting.

EVEN MORE DESSERTS!

Raw Brownies

SERVINGS: 9
PREP/TOTAL TIME: 10 min.

Ingredients

- 1 cup raisins
- 1 cup almonds
- ¼ cup cocoa powder

Instructions

1. Blend raisins, almonds, and cocoa powder in a blender until it turns doughy.
2. Press dough into an 8 x 8 pan.
3. Cut into squares and serve.

Whipped Coconut Cream

SERVINGS: 4
PREP TIME: 10 min.
TOTAL TIME: 8 hours 10 min.

Ingredients

- 1 (14 oz.) can unsweetened coconut milk
- 2 tablespoons white sugar, or to taste
- 1 teaspoon pure vanilla extract

Instructions

1. Refrigerate a can of coconut milk overnight.
2. Before making whipped cream, place metal mixing bowl and beaters in the refrigerator or freezer for 1 hour.
3. Open can of coconut milk, without shaking it. Scoop coconut cream solids into cold mixing bowl. Reserve remaining liquid.
4. Beat coconut cream using electric mixer with chilled beaters on medium speed and then turn to high speed. Continue beating 7 to 8 minutes or until stiff peaks form. Add sugar and vanilla extract and beat another minute.
5. Taste and add more sugar if desired.

Chocolate Almond Cherry Crisps

SERVINGS: 36
PREP TIME: 10 min.
TOTAL TIME: 60 min.

Ingredients

- 1 cup semisweet chocolate chips
- ¾ cup white chocolate chips
- 1½ cups oven-toasted rice cereal (such as Rice Krispies)
- ¾ cup dried cherries
- ⅓ cup slivered almonds
- ½ teaspoon vanilla

Instructions

1. Cover a large baking sheet with wax paper.
2. In a medium microwavable bowl, place semisweet and white chocolate chips. Microwave at HIGH for 45 seconds. Stir, and microwave an additional 45 seconds or until nearly melted. Stir until smooth.
3. Add cereal and remaining ingredients. Quickly stir to combine. Drop mixture by tablespoonful onto baking sheet.
4. Chill for 1 hour or until firm.

Honey Peanut Butter Balls (Gluten-Free)

Ingredients

- ½ cup honey
- ½ cup no sugar added creamy peanut butter
- 2 cups brown rice crispy cereal, crushed
- ½ cup salted peanuts, crushed
- ½ cup chocolate sauce (optional)

Instructions

1. Mix together honey, peanut butter and crushed cereal in a bowl. Roll in crushed peanuts to coat.
2. Place balls on a baking sheet lined with parchment or waxed paper. Refrigerate for 30 minutes.
3. Mix chocolate sauce and refrigerate to thicken slightly, about 15-20 minutes.
4. Dip one ball at a time into chocolate sauce and place on baking sheet.
5. Refrigerate balls for 10-15 minutes until chocolate is hardened.
6. Drizzle with more chocolate sauce on top and chopped peanuts.
7. Keep refrigerated.

Peppermint Patties (Gluten-Free)

SERVINGS: 25
PREP TIME: 20 min.
TOTAL TIME: 1 hour 30 min. + soaking

Ingredients

- ½ cup raw cashews, soaked
- ½ cup coconut oil, melted
- 3-4 tablespoons agave nectar, to taste
- 2 tablespoons almond milk
- 1 teaspoon peppermint extract
- ¾ cup dark chocolate chips
- ½ tablespoon coconut oil

Instructions

1. Place cashews in a bowl and cover with water. Soak for 2-3 hours or overnight for best results.
2. Drain and rinse the cashews.
3. Combine cashews, melted coconut oil, agave, milk, and peppermint extract into a high-speed blender. Blend on high speed until smooth.
4. Line a baking sheet with parchment paper. Add a half tablespoon of filling into a mini cupcake/candy liners. Place on the baking sheet. Repeat until there is no more filling left. Freeze, uncovered, for 20-35 minutes, or until firm.
5. Take the patties out of the cupcake liners and set each on top of their liner. Return to the freezer for 10 minutes to firm up more.
6. Melt the chocolate and coconut oil in a small pot over low heat. When half of the chips are melted, remove from heat and stir until all chips are melted. Allow chocolate to cool for a few minutes.
7. Remove patties from the freezer. With a fork, dunk them in the melted chocolate. Tap the side to shake off excess chocolate and place on parchment paper. Do this quickly so the patties don't melt. If chocolate thickens, reheat chocolate again over low heat.
8. Return patties to the freezer for about 10 minutes or until set and chocolate coating is firm.

Chocolate Pretzel Peanut Butter Squares

SERVINGS: 4
PREP/TOTAL TIME: 15 min. + chilling

Ingredients

- 1½ sticks (12 tablespoons) butter, melted
- 2 cups pretzel rods, crushed into crumbs
- 1½ cups confectioners' sugar
- 1 cup plus 1/4 cup smooth peanut butter
- 1½ cups milk chocolate chips

Instructions

1. In a medium bowl, combine melted butter, pretzel crumbs, confectioners' sugar and 1 cup of the peanut butter. Stir until well mixed.
2. Place the mixture evenly into the bottom of an ungreased 9-by-13-by-2-inch baking dish.
3. In a microwave-safe bowl, combine chocolate chips and the remaining 1/4 cup peanut butter. Microwave in 30-second intervals, stirring in-between, until mixture is smooth and melted, around two intervals. Remove, mix, and then spread over the peanut butter-pretzel.
4. Refrigerate for at least 1 hour.
5. Cut into squares.

Thin Mint Puppy Chow

SERVINGS: 10 cups
PREP TIME: 5 min.
TOTAL TIME: 30 min.

Ingredients

- 16 oz. chocolate bark
- 3.5 oz. Green & Black's mint Chocolate Bar
- 2 cups powdered sugar
- 10 cups Rice Chex cereal
- 1 bag (8oz) mint M&M candies

Instructions

1. In a microwave, melt all the chocolates for one minute. Stir and continue melting in 30 second intervals until smooth (approximately 2 minutes).
2. In a large mixing bowl, combine cereal with melted chocolate. Folding with a large wooden spoon until cereal is completely coated.
3. In a large, gallon sized Ziploc bag, add powdered sugar. Spoon in chocolate cereal mix. Seal bag and shake until powdered sugar has coated the cereal completely. Pour onto a large piece of wax paper and allow chocolate to set (about 20 minutes).
4. Combine candies with Chex and store in an airtight container.

Lemon Vanilla Energy Balls

SERVINGS: 20 balls
PREP/ TOTAL TIME: 15 min.

Ingredients

- 1 cup raw almonds
- 1 cup pitted dates
- ½ cup vanilla protein powder
- 2 teaspoons maca powder (optional)
- ½ teaspoons sea salt
- zest, 1 lemon
- juice, ½ lemon

Instructions

1. Add almonds to a food processor. Blend until it reaches a crumbly consistency.
2. Add in dates, protein powder and maca powder. Process until combined.
3. Add in sea salt, lemon zest and juice and continue processing until mix comes together into one big sticky ball.
4. Break up into 20 pieces and roll pieces into balls.
5. Store in refrigerator.

Peanut Butter Balls (Gluten-Free)

SERVINGS: 16-20
PREP TIME: 15 min.
TOTAL TIME: 40 min.

Ingredients

- 1 cup 100% natural peanut butter (smooth or crunchy)
- 3½-4 tablespoons pure maple syrup, to taste
- 2-3 tablespoons coconut flour
- ¼ teaspoon fine grain sea salt
- 6 tablespoons gluten-free rice crisp cereal
- ¾ cup dark chocolate chips
- ½ tablespoon coconut oil

Instructions

1. Stir peanut butter jar very well. In a large bowl, mix peanut butter and maple syrup vigorously, for 30-60 seconds or until it thickens.
2. Stir in coconut flour. Let sit for a few minutes until firm. Add some more coconut flour if necessary, or more syrup if it's too dry.
3. Add salt in the cereal. Stir.
4. Shape into small balls.
5. In a small pot, add chocolate chips and coconut oil. Heat over low heat, stirring frequently. Once half the chips have melted, remove from heat and stir until smooth.
6. With a fork, dip balls into the melted chocolate. Place ball on a plate or cutting board lined with parchment. Repeat for all balls. Set aside any leftover chocolate.
7. Place balls in the freezer for 6-8 minutes or until mostly firm.
8. Dip a fork into the leftover melted chocolate and drizzle it on top of the balls to create a fancy design.
9. Freeze the balls for 10-15 minutes or until the chocolate is completely set.

Peanut Butter Chocolate Haystacks

SERVINGS: 24 pieces
PREP TIME: 10 min.
TOTAL TIME: 2 hours

Ingredients

- 12 oz. pkg. semi-sweet chocolate morsels
- 11 oz. pkg. butterscotch morsels
- ½ cup creamy peanut butter
- 1 cup dry salted peanuts
- 3 cup Chow Mein noodles
- 8 oz. pkg. mini Reese's Peanut Butter Cups

Instructions

1. In a large microwave safe bowl, melt semi-sweet morsels with butterscotch and peanut butter for 1 minute. Stir and microwave an additional 30 seconds. Stir again until smooth, or heat an additional 30 seconds.
2. Add peanuts and Chow Mein noodles to the melted mixture.
3. Pour mix into a 9 inch parchment paper lined baking dish. Press peanut butter cups on top and refrigerate for 2 hours.

Thin Mints

SERVINGS: 15
PREP TIME: 15 min.
TOTAL TIME: 30 min.

Ingredients

- 15 Chocolate Wafers
- 8 oz. Semi-Sweet Baking Chocolate (8 squares)
- ¼-½ teaspoons peppermint extract (or oil)

Instructions

1. Line a baking sheet with parchment or waxed paper.
2. Chop chocolate into small pieces
3. Place chocolate into a small microwave safe bowl. Microwave on high for 60 seconds. Stir chocolate and microwave again in 15 second bursts, stirring in between, until most of chocolate is melted. Avoid overheating the chocolate.
4. Stir in peppermint extract. Start with ¼ teaspoon and add a touch more if you like.
5. Dip the cookies using a fork gently in chocolate and coat on both sides. Let excess chocolate drip off before setting cookies down on the baking sheet.
6. Let set at room temperature, and store in the refrigerator.

Sunflower and Pumpkin Seed Energy Balls

SERVINGS: 10
PREP TIME: 15 min.
TOTAL TIME: 30 min.

Ingredients

- 1 cup old fashioned oats
- ½ cup ground flax seed
- ½ cup peanut butter
- ⅓ cup honey
- 1-2 teaspoons vanilla
- ½ cup chocolate chips
- ¼ cup sunflower seeds
- ⅛ cup raw pumpkin seeds

Instructions

1. Combine all ingredients into a bowl and mix with spoon until combined.
2. Place in refrigerator for at least 30 minutes to firm.
3. Roll into 1 inch balls.
4. Place back in refrigerator in an airtight container until ready to eat.

THANK YOU

Thank you for checking out my Vegan No-Bake Desserts Cookbook. I hope you enjoyed these recipes as much as I have. I am always looking for feedback on how to improve, so if you have any questions, suggestions, or comments please send me an email at susan.evans.author@gmail.com. Also, if you enjoyed the book would you consider leaving on honest review? As a new author, they help me out in a big way. Thanks again, and have fun cooking!

Other popular books by Susan Evans

Quick & Easy Vegan Desserts Cookbook:
Over 80 delicious recipes for cakes, cupcakes, brownies, cookies, fudge, pies, candy, and so much more!

Quick & Easy Microwave Meals:
Over 50 recipes for breakfast, snacks, meals and desserts

Quick & Easy Asian Vegetarian Cookbook:
Over 50 recipes for stir fries, rice, noodles, and appetizers

Vegetarian Mediterranean Cookbook:
Over 50 recipes for appetizers, salads, dips, and main dishes

The Vegetarian DASH Diet Cookbook:
Over 100 recipes for breakfast, lunch, dinner and sides!

The Complete Rice Cooker Meals Cookbook Bundle:
Over 100 recipes for breakfast, main dishes, soups, and desserts!

Vegetarian Slow Cooker Cookbook:
Over 75 recipes for meals, soups, stews, desserts, and sides

Halloween Cookbook:
80 Ghoulish recipes for appetizers, meals, drinks, and desserts

Printed in Poland
by Amazon Fulfillment
Poland Sp. z o.o., Wrocław

52383906R00059